Facebook
and Mark Zuckerberg

· Business Leaders ·

Facebook and Mark Zuckerberg

Judy L. Hasday

MORGAN REYNOLDS
PUBLISHING

Greensboro, North Carolina

To my mom, for her lifetime of love,
friendship, and support. I love you.
And to my River Sisters—"paddles up"

Mark Zuckerberg, founder and CEO of Facebook, delivers the keynote address during the annual Facebook f8 developer conference in San Francisco in 2008.

le the power to
make the world
n and connected

Business Leaders
Facebook and Mark Zuckerberg
Copyright © 2012 by Morgan Reynolds Publishing

Library of Congress Cataloging-in-Publication Data

Hasday, Judy L., 1957-
 Facebook and Mark Zuckerberg / by Judy L. Hasday.
    p. cm. -- (Business leaders)
 Includes bibliographical references and index.
 ISBN 978-1-59935-176-6 (alk. paper) -- ISBN 978-1-59935-215-2
(e-book :
alk. paper)
 1. Zuckerberg, Mark, 1984- 2. Facebook (Firm)--Juvenile litera-
ture. 3.
Facebook (Electronic resource)--Juvenile literature. 4.
Webmasters--United
States--Biography--Juvenile literature. 5. Online social
networks--Juvenile literature. 6. Internet industry--United
States--Juvenile literature. I. Title.
 HM743.F33Z843 2012
 006.7'54092--dc23
 [B]
                                        2011023210

Printed in the United States of America
First Edition

Book cover and interior designed by:
Ed Morgan, navyblue design studio
Greensboro, NC

Table of Contents

Chapter One: Techno Kid   11

Chapter Two: More than Just a Geek   21

Chapter Three: Hacking Harvard   33

Chapter Four: Whose Idea Was It?   45

Chapter Five: Palo Alto: A "Mythical Place"   61

Chapter Six: The World's Biggest Social Network   77

Chapter Seven: Facebook's Global Influence   93

Timeline   103
Sources   104
Bibliography   107
Web sites   108
Index   109

CHAPTER ONE

Techno Kid

Mark Zuckerberg's parents thought he would grow up and become a lawyer. From an early age, it was obvious that Mark was smart, creative, and determined. He was also "strong willed and relentless," his father, Edward Zuckerberg, recalled.

"For some kids, their questions could be answered with a simple yes or no. For Mark, if he asked for something, yes by itself would work, but no required much more. If you were going to say no to him, you had better be prepared with a strong argument backed by facts, experiences, logic, reasons. We envisioned him becoming a lawyer one day, with a near 100% success rate of convincing juries."

Although his parents may have thought he'd become a lawyer, Mark's interests were devoted more to computers and technology. At Harvard, he used those interests to create Facebook, which has transformed the way people connect with one another. What started out as an online directory to connect college students has exploded into an international global network, with more than 145 million Facebook users living in the United States. And Mark accomplished this by combining his personal philosophy of trying to make the world a more open place with his love of computers and technology.

Born in White Plains, New York, on May 14, 1984, Mark Elliot Zuckerberg is the second child and only son of Edward and Karen Zuckerberg. Edward was an oral surgeon and Karen had a psychiatry practice until she stopped working in order to raise her children.

Edward and Karen had four children. In addition to Mark there is Randi, the oldest, Donna, and Arielle.

Not long after Mark was born the Zuckerberg family moved from White Plains to the nearby village of Dobbs Ferry, which is located in Westchester County, New York, just a few miles west of the Hudson River. The village has been a popular location site for shooting Hollywood films including *Unfaithful, Michael Collins,* and *Falling in Love.*

The Zuckerbergs bought a single home near the Juhring Estate, a seventy-six acre woodland preserve that offers residents unspoiled hiking, walking, and biking trails. Nature lovers can go bird-watching, and everyone can feel safe in a community that has very minimal crime. The Zuckerberg family home also housed Edward's dental office. Not surprising to note that as the father of an Internet phenom, Edward has his own Web site for his practice. Known by his patients as "painless Dr. Z.," he had a 155-gallon salt-water aquarium built into the wall of his treatment room. Edward still practices and is still concerned about his patient's comfort. He even offers iPods with a large enough musical selection to choose from for his patients to listen to during treatment.

In 1985, when his son was just a year old, Edward began computerizing his office, although he had limited knowledge of technology. In a radio interview with Paul Feiner on WVOX in New Rochelle, New York, he said:

> I've always been technologically oriented in the office, I've always had the latest high-tech toys, if you want to call them, and my office was computerized very early on; I was one of the first dental offices in the country to have computerization back in 1985. So my kids all grew up around the office and were all exposed to computers and had the advantage of being exposed to the technology early on, so that certainly enriched the development of Mark's affinity for the technology.

Edward had an early model of the Atari 800 and showed his young son how to do Atari BASIC computer programming. BASIC is an acronym for Beginner's All-purpose Symbolic Instruction Code. Originally designed in 1964 by John Kemeny and Thomas Kurtz at Dartmouth College in Hanover, New Hampshire,

BASIC permitted non-mathematicians and scientists a way to write software.

It didn't take long for Mark to begin demonstrating his computer know-how. He started his computer training on a Quantex 486DX that ran on Windows 3.1. One day in 1996, Edward was trying to figure out a better way for a patient's arrival to be announced in the office. Mark, then just twelve years old, created a software program that allowed all of the computers in the house to communicate with his father's office. Though rather primitive by today's technology, Mark's program, dubbed ZuckNet, enabled users to send messages back and forth to any computer linked by the software. A "ping" sound from the ZuckNet application from the receptionist to Edward advised him of the arrival of a patient. From his office Edward could also "ping" back and forth with wife Karen and the children on any of the computers in the house.

Mark acknowledged in his *Time* 2010 Person of the Year interview that he needed the help of a professional to wire up the family network, but he did all the programming. What Mark created with ZuckNet was similar to an AOL Instant Messenger (IM)-type program, minus the ability to type words.

Mark would sometimes use ZuckNet to pull pranks on his family. His sister Donna tells the story of how one night, while she was working in her room, a message popped up on her computer screen warning of a deadly virus that was going to blow up in thirty seconds. While the numbers on the screen counted down, from thirty, Donna yelled for Mark to come help.

Mark's sisters were often in on his pranks. As the year 2000 approached there was great international concern about the world's computer systems. The problem was dubbed the Y2K bug (Y for "year,", and k for the SI unit prefix kilo meaning 1000; hence, 2K signifies 2000). Many computer programs stored calendar years with only two decimal digits. For example, 1980 was stored as 80. The question was would a program be able to distinguish between 1900 and 2000 since both ended in double zero? There were dire concerns about what such a problem could do to the world's infrastructure.

Hewlett Packard CEO Carly Fiorina, center, gets a tour of the Y2K Command Center at Hewlett Packard headquarters in Palo Alto, California, on December 31, 1999.

Would crucial utilities such as nuclear power plants shut down? Would bank records be lost? Would electricity shut off leaving everyone in the dark? Fortunately, except for a few isolated problems, the Y2K fears were unfounded. Still, Mark and his sister Randi waited for the hands of the clock to hit midnight on New Year's Eve 1999 to play a practical joke on the family by turning the power off in the house.

Mark was born at the right time for someone who was so naturally gifted in creating in the world of computers and other emerging technologies. For example, the Internet Protocol Suite (TCP/IP), the necessary communications protocols for exchanging messages between computers, was standardized in 1982.

Mark was not yet in high school when Google was launched and for most of his youth was able to message someone. By the time he entered high school the Internet had become part of many people's daily lives. Unlike Bill Gates and other personal computer pioneers, Mark came of age when computers and the Internet were transforming our lives.

Edward and Karen recognized early on that Mark would need to be challenged intellectually. He would need to "play" with the technology and be free to explore its capabilities. They couldn't have known what the impact of his early tinkering and creating would lead to and how it would change the way people would communicate, but their support and encouragement of his fascination with all things digital was critical to his future success.

CHAPTER
TWO

More Than Just a Geek

Though younger than his sister, Randi, Mark easily beat her at video games, such as the Japanese-designed Nintendo games Mario Brothers and Mario Kart. Randi felt that Mark was always thinking nine to ten steps ahead of her.

Long before the virtual capabilities of games like Wii, there were console systems like Nintendo and Sega that accepted a variety of programmed cartridges that housed dozens of video games. Many of these games had multilevel challenges to complete in order to win the game.

A Nintendo 64 game
console and controller

Even though Mark enjoyed playing computer games, he delighted even more in creating his own. "I had a bunch of friends who were artists." he said. "They'd come over, draw stuff, and I'd build a game out of it."

He also had a vivid, creative imagination. Among his favorite books is one titled *Ender's Game*, a science-fiction novel by Orson Scott Card. The central character, Andrew (Ender) Wiggin, is a boy who is trained to play computer war "games" but soon realizes that he is in the middle of a real life or death war battle. Ender is a genius, a true whiz kid who wins every "game" by mastering his ability to maneuver around on a computer.

Edward and Karen encouraged their children to pursue whatever interested them. "Probably the best thing I can say is something that my wife and I have always believed in," Edward said. "Rather than impose upon your kids or try and steer their lives in a certain direction, to recognize what their strengths are and support their strengths and support the development of the things they're passionate about."

Mark was more interested in playing around on the computer than he was almost anything else, so when he was eleven his parents hired a computer expert to tutor him at home. Edward and Karen enlisted the help of software developer David Newman, who came to the Zuckerberg house once a week to work with Mark. Newman soon recognized that he was not tutoring a youngster who had a mere interest in technology. Newman sometimes had difficulty keeping up with Mark. He believed Mark was a prodigy, a young man with a tremendous intellectual gift. Home tutoring was soon replaced with a Thursday night graduate-level computer course at Mercy College in Dobbs Ferry. Mark was so much younger than the other students that the class instructor at first thought Edward was bringing his son to class with him, not dropping him off.

After attending Springhurst Elementary School, pre-teen Mark continued his studies at Dobbs Ferry Middle School. At thirteen, he had his Bar Mitzvah at Temple Beth Abraham in Tarrytown, New York. A huge *Star Wars* fan, Mark had a *Star Wars*-themed reception afterward. He loved the movie so much he even filmed a parody of it during one winter school break. Titled "Star Wars Sill-ogy," the production was serious business. Sister Randi remembered that Mark even called production meetings in the morning before starting the day's filming.

Mark, of course, was Luke Skywalker, hero of the *Star Wars* saga. Randi couldn't remember which sister, Donna or Arielle, was drafted into service to portray R2D2, but she did remember the costume—an over-turned garbage can. Mark also continued to write computer programs, mostly games like a variation on Monopoly and an adaptation of the game Risk, a game whose goal is to achieve world domination.

Mark spent ninth and tenth grade at Ardsley High School. However, by the end of his sophomore year, his life changed. He was accepted to the prestigious Phillips Exeter Academy, a private boarding school in Exeter, New Hampshire. He chose the school because of its excellent reputation in the fields of computers and mathematics.

Philips Exeter is about fifty miles north of Boston and about 250 miles from Dobbs Ferry. Founded in 1781, the school "has a tradition of academic excellence, a distinguished faculty, and a long history of educating young people to find their place in the world."

The library at Phillips Exeter

Exeter has a very informal classroom learning environment, and students have their choice of 450 classes from which they can design their own course of study. With nineteen departments, including everything from anthropology, English, and mathematics, to classical and modern languages and theater and dance, students have a wealth of subjects to choose to study. Students can also take part in more than one hundred clubs, sixty-six athletic teams in twenty different sports, and more than fifteen performance troupes.

At Exeter, Mark showed a strong aptitude for the classical languages—both Greek and Latin. He enjoyed the classical languages so much that at the end of his junior year at Exeter he attended a three-month intensive summer school course in ancient Greek at Harvard University. He also joined the Fencing Club. Soon he was a skilled fencer with a highly competitive nature. During a regional competition of the U.S. Fencing Association in New York in 2000, he was voted the Most Valuable Player, a rare achievement for someone so young.

Both his interest in ancient languages and in an old world combat form seemed at odds with his passion for modern technology. But he had a variety of interests that he was able to explore within the Exeter experience.

The Olympic Men's Individual Epee event at the Helliniko
Fencing Hall just outside Athens, Greece, in 2004

He joined the math team, of course, as well as the science Olympiad and the Latin honors society.

Despite all of his extracurricular activities, tooling around with computers was always a part of Mark's day. He liked to think of ways to work more efficiently and would sometimes share what he'd created with other students. He created a Web site with classmate Kristopher Tillery that enabled Exeter students to order a variety of munchies online. For his senior year project Mark and classmate Adam D'Angelo wrote "software for an MP3 player that was able to learn a user's listening habits and build a digital library based on previous selections." They called the software Synapse. As was the case with ZuckNet, which was a precursor to AOL Instant Messenger, Synapse was the forerunner of today's Pandora. Synapse allowed the user to discover music that they were not familiar with and build digital libraries of the music that appealed to them.

"The playlist ran out on my computer, and I thought, 'You know, there's really no reason why my computer shouldn't just know what I want to learn next.' So that's what we made," said Mark, explaining the thinking behind Synapse.

Since the Internet provides the instant dispatch of information, news of the software was soon showing up on technology blogs. When reviewed on Slashdot, a Web site that bills itself as a place for "News for Nerds," Synapse earned a three out of five rating from *PC Magazine*. Eventually, Microsoft and AOL approached Mark to buy the software program, offering $1 million for Synapse. They also wanted to hire Mark and Adam to further develop the capabilities of the software. Mark turned down the offer. At the time, he wasn't thinking about money. "I don't really like putting a price-tag on the stuff I do. That's just like not the point," he says.

As he approached graduation from Phillips Exeter Academy, Mark wanted to be among the group of newly accepted freshmen at Harvard University. On his application he noted that he had won prizes in science, math, astronomy and physics, and classical studies. He was also fluent in several languages, including French, Hebrew, Latin, and ancient Greek. Referring back to his love of fencing, Mark wrote that the sport had, "proven to be the perfect medium" because "whether I am competing against a rival in a USFA tournament or just clashing foils, or sometimes sabers, with a friend, I rarely find myself doing anything more enjoyable than fencing a good bout."

Applying to Harvard, one of the best and most competitive universities in the country, could mean that Mark would no longer stand out from his classmates—he'd be just another intelligent freshman. However, the buzz about his creations at Exeter preceded him.

In the fall of 2002, Mark stepped onto the Ivy League campus with a reputation as a computer programming aficionado. With his ZuckNet design and Synapse program on his resume, he had more than demonstrated a gifted aptitude at working with the technology that was defining his generation.

Memorial Hall at Harvard University

CHAPTER
THREE

Hacking Harvard

There was nothing especially noticeable about Mark when he made his way across the Harvard campus except the fact he wore white socks under his open-toe Adidas sandals everywhere he went. He was not a looming presence at five feet eight inches tall. His favorite dress attire consisted of t-shirts and jeans and a fleece hoodie. However, he would soon make his mark at the prestigious university.

Harvard University

With his passion for technology, majoring in computer science would seem to have been the obvious choice for Mark. As he later said in an interview with the *Harvard Crimson*, "I'm just like a little kid. I get bored easily and computers excite me." However, he chose to work toward a double major in computer science and psychology. To Mark, it was a natural link. He believed that computers could enable people to connect more easily and as a result would help them to better understand each other.

Mark has admitted that he was not the easiest guy to befriend. He even wrote on his Harvard application that his sense of humor was sometimes obnoxious. He did join the Jewish fraternity, Alpha Epsilon Pi, and moved into his room in one of the first-year students' dormitories. But instead of socializing he spent his free hours pursuing what he most enjoyed—writing computer code in his dorm room.

Mark often wore a t-shirt with an image of an ape on it with the words "code monkey," which is a slang term for an overworked software programmer. Mark's self-depreciating sense of humor was also evident in a set of beer glasses he had in his room. The type on the glasses read: "pound include beer dot H." It was a tag for C++ programming code: #include beer.h.

In Mark's sophomore year at Harvard, he moved into Suite H33 at the Kirkland House, one of the upperclassmen living quarters shared by almost five hundred students. The House has several facilities, including a gym, lounge, game room, two music rooms, and a dining hall that boasts some of the best food on campus. Kirkland House had been a favorite of the school jocks, but that had changed when a lottery system was implemented to assign rooms to upperclassmen.

Usually four to six students were assigned to a room or suite, depending on its size. Mark shared his room with Chris Hughes, who was raised in Hickory, North Carolina, and had attended Phillips Academy in Andover, Massachusetts. Chris would go on to earn his bachelor's degree in history and literature. Because the room had bunk beds, and neither of them wanted to sleep on the top bunk, they dismantled the frame and put the mattresses on the floor next to one another.

Other Kirkland residents who became Mark's friends included Dustin Moscovitz and Eduardo Saverin. Dustin was an economics major who was raised in Ocala, Florida. Eduardo, a Brazilian American, was born in São Paulo, Brazil, and raised in Miami, Florida. Eduardo came from a very affluent family. His father was a Brazilian entrepreneur who made his fortune in several businesses, including export, clothing, shipping, and real estate. He was also a fraternity brother at Alpha Epsilon Pi. Eduardo was also known around campus for having made an estimated $300,000 by being able to determine weather patterns. He then bought oil company stocks by using his analysis to judge when heating oil would be at its greatest demand. Like Dustin, Eduardo was an economics major.

Kirkland House at Harvard

Whether it was the move to Kirkland House, his new roommates, or just the right "time," Mark became more active on campus. He created software programs that he shared with others. For example, once he explained what he'd done in one evening. "Half the things I do I don't release," he explained. "I spent five hours programming last night, and came up with something that was kind of cool, showed it to a bunch of my friends, and the rest of campus will never know about it."

When he wasn't focused on writing code, Mark occasionally took in a fraternity party on campus or a function going on with Alpha Epsilon Pi. According to roommate Arie Hasit, who was also a member of Alpha Epsilon Pi, Mark would wander over to the Hillel House (Harvard Hillel) where he could meet up with other Jewish students and participate in activities there. Hillel's mission "is to provide every Jewish Harvard student—without regard to ideological commitment or background—appropriate

The Coat of Arms of Alpha Epsilon Pi

grounding for making meaningful Jewish choices in a complex and changing world."

In the summer of 2003, between his freshman and sophomore year at Harvard, Mark had begun to spend time hanging out with friends who also liked to play around with software ideas. He also had a job coding Web sites, which meant he was earning money doing work that for him wasn't really "work" at all. Earlier that year Mark's high school best friend and Synapse co-creator Adam D'Angelo, who was attending the California Institute of Technology (CalTech), had invented a program he called Buddy Zoo. The program allowed users to list "their friends and compared their list to those their friends had uploaded. What resulted was a rudimentary social network—a set of connections between people. Buddy Zoo grew to several hundred thousand users within months then D'Angelo let it die. It was merely an experiment."

In subsequent conversations between the friends, they started to wonder why it had become popular so fast. Mark decided it was because the Internet was changing into a medium that would make it easier for people to develop social connections.

When Mark started the fall semester of his sophomore year, he created a Web site he called Course

Match that helped students pick classes based on who else was enrolling in them. For example, if an acquaintance in your chemistry class was someone you wanted to get to know better, you could then look up a psychology class, for example, to see if he or she were taking that class the following semester. Course Match was an instant hit online. Almost over night several hundred users were accessing it. A few weeks later, Mark created something that was even more popular and perhaps more invasive of one's privacy.

On the evening of October 28, 2003, Mark returned to Kirkland House a bit inebriated and annoyed. He sat down at his computer and wrote in his blog:

> Jessica A— is a bitch. I need to think of something to take my mind off her. I need to think of something to occupy my mind. Easy enough, now I just need an idea.

> An hour later: I'm a little intoxicated, not gonna lie. So what if it's not even 10 p.m. and it's a Tuesday night? What? The Kirkland [dorm] facebook is open on my desktop and some of these people have

pretty horrendous facebook pics. I almost want to put some of these faces next to pictures of farm animals and have people vote on which is more attractive.

At 11:09 p.m., invention was in full swing: Yea, it's on. I'm not exactly sure how the farm animals are going to fit into this whole thing (you can't really ever be sure with farm animals . . .), but I like the idea of comparing two people together.

Fortunately, roommate Billy Olsen convinced Mark not to use farm animals. Mark named the project on his blog, "Harvard Face Mash: The Process." It became known as Facemash.com. The idea was to find out who were the "hottest" people on campus. Mark hacked into the Harvard University computer directory where all of the current students were listed and downloaded each student's identification photograph. Then he programmed the Web site so that it randomly brought up two different photos of the same sex at the same time. Users could compare the two faces and vote on who was the best looking.

"Zuckerberg hacked into the night, breaking into the private user data of each of Harvard's residences and blogging proudly about his exploits every step of the way," wrote Claire Hoffman in her *Rolling Stone* article "The Battle for Facebook." "The site was an instant hit."

Hoffman added, "That first night, students across campus were e-mailing one another about Facemash. More than 450 signed up, logging 22,000 page views. Within hours, school officials tracked down Zuckerberg and shut off his Web access. Later, in a hearing before Harvard's administrators, he was accused of violating student privacy and downloading school property without permission."

Mark later apologized for hurting anyone, saying it was unintentional, and also apologized to the Harvard University administration for violating school rules. He admitted that he had failed to consider both the possibility the site would become so popular so quickly or that it was an invasion of his fellow student's privacy.

The notoriety from the Facemash.com incident gave Mark an identity on campus. He was the guy who hacked into the Harvard University network database. He had put up something live that people responded to in a much bigger and faster way than he could have imagined. Perhaps the most crucial lesson Mark learned from creating Facemash.com was something he later said in a court deposition: "People," he summarized, "are more voyeuristic than what I would have thought." He tucked this knowledge about human behavior away in his mind for future reference.

CHAPTER
FOUR

Whose Idea Was It?

On November 7, 2003, Mark met a Chinese American student from Braintree, Massachusetts, while at an Alpha Epsilon Pi fraternity party. The two were in line for the bathroom and while waiting they struck up a conversation. Priscilla Chan was a premed student majoring in biology at Harvard. Mark was wearing one of his "geek" t-shirts so Priscilla assumed he was a computer guy. "He was this nerdy guy who was just a little bit out there," said Chan about her first impression of Mark. The two began dating.

Mark created things on the computer for a variety of reasons. Sometimes it was because he was bored. Sometimes it was because he liked to tinker around writing code. Sometimes it was as a result of making his life a little easier.

The fall semester of his sophomore year had been a busy one. Finding himself two days away from a final exam in his art history class, Mark realized he hadn't allowed enough time to study. The exam required each student to discuss five hundred images from the Augustan period in history (30 BCE–CE 14). "This isn't the kind of thing where you can just go in and figure out how to do it, like calculus or math," he says, without a trace of irony. "You actually have to learn these things ahead of time." So he did what he knew how to do best—he designed a Web site with one image on a page and added an area to post comments about the image. To get the page activity, he e-mailed the other students in the class and invited them to share their notes. What Mark created was essentially an online study group. In just a few hours, all the images on the site had notes written and shared by the classmates. Mark did well on the exam and so did the other students who had participated in the study group.

Mark's Facemash site had caught the attention of three Harvard upperclassmen—Divya Narendra and twin brothers Cameron and Tyler Winklevoss. Divya was an applied mathematics major who had grown up in Bayside, Queens, New York. Both of his parents were physicians and when he was young Divya thought about following in his parents' footsteps. He posted a near perfect score on his SATs while a student at Townsend Harris High School and was accepted to Harvard for the fall semester in 2000. Cameron and Tyler grew up in Greenwich, a very affluent town in Connecticut.

ConnectU founders Tyler Winklevoss, left, and Cameron Winklevoss, right, with Divya Narendra

Their father, Howard E. Winklevoss, Ph D was a professor at the prestigious Wharton School of Business at the University of Pennsylvania. Even as children the twins worked as a team and as young teens taught themselves HyperText Markup Language (HTML). They launched a company building Web sites for businesses. At Harvard they were rowers on the Harvard crew team.

The 2004 Harvard crew team

Divya, Tyler, and Cameron lived at Pforzheimer House, one of the undergraduate residential houses on the Harvard campus. In December of 2002 the three friends began drafting a plan to create a Web site that would make it easier for Harvard students to connect with one another and with students at other universities. There would be a section where students searching for dates could upload photos and profiles. The other part of the Web site would be a place where students could network in order to exchange information about classes, look for jobs, or simply hang out. "All three of us were fairly excited about . . . the idea," Divya remembered later. "I [knew] it had potential to be something that was really big and something that we could down the road make money on." Divya said that the project "was intended to be a collection of profiles of individuals who wanted to get to know other individuals . . . at Harvard or abroad or outside of Harvard." They called the Web site HarvardConnection.

The HarvardConnection trio decided they needed an ace code programmer to finish the work. All three also agreed that whoever they brought on to the project would be offered an equal share of the partnership and an equal financial share of whatever the eventual Web site generated. Divya remembered Mark's exploits with Facemash and in early November sent him an e-mail: "We're very deep into developing a site which we would like you to be a part of and . . . which we know will make some waves on campus."

Mark was, according to Divya, Tyler, Cameron and Victor Gao—one of the original Harvard Connection programmers—very enthusiastic about coming onboard and finishing up the work to get HarvardConnection launched. He began working to finish the code. Towards the end of November, Mark e-mailed Victor and Divya to update them on his progress: "I have most of the coding done, and I think that once I get the graphics we'll be able to launch this thing."

However, this e-mail was the last meaningful communication from Mark for several days. According to Divya, Tyler, and Cameron, Mark continued to postpone scheduling meetings, didn't answer his cell phone or respond to e-mails.

Finally, in December, Mark met with Divya, Tyler, and Cameron in his dorm room at Kirkland House. He reiterated his interest in the project and even had code scribbled on a whiteboard in his room with the title HarvardConnection scrawled across the top. What Mark didn't tell them was that he was working on his own "social networking" site. On January 11, 2004, three days before he had a final meeting with Divya and the twins to tell them he was ending his work with HarvardConnection, Mark paid thirty-five dollars to register the original Facebook site, which he called TheFacebook.com. He had been busy building his site instead of finishing the HarvardConnection project.

Mark spent the last few weeks in January writing code. He was in a hurry to launch TheFacebook.com. According to friends and roommates, Mark didn't eat, sleep, or talk to anyone while he was programming during the final stretch at the end of January 2004. He had told a few friends about the project, including Eduardo Saverin, Dustin Moskovitz, Chris Hughes, and Arie Hasit.

On February 4 TheFacebook.com ("The" was dropped in 2005) was launched to the students at Harvard. On its home screen Mark left a message for people coming to the site: "Thefacebook is an online directory that connects people through social networks at colleges. We have opened up Thefacebook for popular consumption at Harvard University. You can use Thefacebook to: Search for people at your school; Find out who are in your classes; Look up your friends' friends; See a visualization of your social network."

Mark told his dorm mates to sign up. The first three accounts were dummy accounts, so Mark was user number four. Chris signed up as five, Dustin was number six, and Eduardo became the seventh user. In an interview with Guy Grimland of "Haaretz.com," Arie Hasit shared how the launch occurred:

Mark came to me on the day he built Facebook, and he said to me, 'Arie, I built this site. I want you to sign up.' And that is how I signed up to Facebook. I put a favorite quote of mine in the profile. I specified my favorite books, which courses I take at Harvard. I uploaded one picture to the profile. . . . Initially Zuckerberg asked a small group of people to sign up to Facebook. At a certain point he told us to start inviting friends, and that is what we did on the first and second day which the site went up on the Web. We could only invite students enrolled at Harvard. In fact, if you did not have a Harvard e-mail address you could not sign into Facebook.

The site caught on almost immediately, boasting 4,000 users within the first two weeks. Some used it as a social site to connect, flirt, and have fun. Others used it for more practical purposes such as creating study groups for classes, posting the names of clubs and organizations students could join, and locations and times for parties. Mark enlisted Dustin to work on

Mark in
2005

expanding the Web site
to other college cam-
puses. Chris became
the official spokesman
and handled all interview requests. Eduardo provided
an initial $1,000 for marketing and additional money
when needed to purchase servers to handle all the traffic
the site was receiving. Because of Eduardo's education
in economics he was also tasked with running the business side. Soon TheFacebook had expanded to three
other Ivy League schools.

While Mark and his partners were reveling in the
phenomenal success of TheFacebook, Divya, Tyler,

and Cameron were stunned and angry. They found out about the Web site the Monday after it launched by reading about it in a *Harvard Crimson* press release. On February 10, Mark received a letter from the trio accusing him of violating their agreement and stealing their idea. In an e-mail response Mark addressed the accusations. "Originally, I was intrigued by the project and was asked to finish the Connect (Professional) side of the Web site. I did this," the e-mail read. Zuckerberg went on to say after their January 14 meeting, he began working on his own site, "using none of the same code nor functionality that is present in HarvardConnection" and that "this was a separate venture, and did not draw on any of the ideas discussed in our meetings."

But Victor, disagreed with Mark's explanation. He had taken a second look at Mark's work and came to the conclusion that "Mark's 'work' on the site amounted to about two hours of essentially a search-and-replace operation over the existing code I had written."

The Winklevoss brothers filed a grievance with the Harvard administration board, citing the Honor Code, which "expects that all students will be honest and forthcoming in their dealings with the members of this community." The board refused to hear the case. The Winklevosses next wrote a letter to Harvard president Lawrence Summers. He, too, declined to get involved in the matter, saying it was not within the university's jurisdiction.

Lawrence Summers

While seeking what they considered to be a fair resolution to the conflict with Mark, the HarvardConnection trio moved ahead with their project. They renamed it ConnectU and launched the site on May 21, 2004. ConnectU didn't attract users as quickly as TheFacebook. By September, Facebook had approximately 285,000 users at ninety-nine colleges and universities. ConnectU had about 15,000 users.

On September 2, 2004, Divya Narendra, and Cameron and Tyler Winklevoss filed a federal lawsuit in Massachusetts "claiming Zuckerberg stole their concept while working on code for the Harvard graduates' version of an online social networking service."

Tyler Winklevoss, front, and Cameron Winklevoss arrive for a news conference in Boston in July 2007.

At this time Mark was probably not even aware of the on-going pursuits of Divya and the Winklevoss brothers. At the end of the spring semester, he decided to pack his bags and head west to Palo Alto, California. To Mark, the Silicon Valley, where Apple Computer and many of the other computer technology and Internet businesses had been founded, was the best place to go to try to take Facebook national.

Mark was following in the footsteps of Bill Gates who, nearly thirty years before, had left Harvard before graduation to launch his software company, Microsoft.

Social Networking Before Facebook

Major active social networking Web sites were appearing on the World Wide Web as early as 1995. The top three social networking sites launched before Facebook were Classmates.com (1995), Friendster (2002), and LinkedIn (May 2003). All three had unique aspects that attracted users.

Classmates.com was created by Randy Conrads "to assist members in finding friends and acquaintances from kindergarten, primary school, high school, college, work and the United States military." The site has 50 million registered users, who can access other information that has a more nostalgic focus including old yearbooks, photos, and music tracks. In 2010 the site was renamed Memory Lane.

Friendster was founded in the United States, but today most of its registered users—115 million to date—are located in Asia, especially in the

Philippines, Indonesia, Malaysia, India, and Singapore. The site gets about 19 billion views a month and is used for dating, sharing photos, and communicating with other members. Of the three sites, Friendster is most like the early versions of Facebook.

LinkedIn is probably the most unlike the other three networks because it was created as a business networking site for professionals. With more than 100 million registered users globally, "LinkedIn can be used to find jobs, people and business opportunities recommended by someone in one's contact network. Employers can list jobs and search for potential candidates. Job seekers can review the profile of hiring managers and discover which of their existing contacts can introduce them." About half of LinkedIn's users are in the United States (44 million), and the rest (56 million) are in countries around the world.

CHAPTER
FIVE

Palo Alto: A "Mythical Place"

Before Mark could expand Facebook he needed to have a clear understanding of what made the site so appealing. It certainly had appealed to the college-age demographic. One Harvard student later said that "While Facebook isn't explicitly about bringing people together in romantic unions, there are plenty of other primal instincts evident at work here: an element of wanting to belong, a dash of vanity and more than a little voyeurism." Now Mark had to see if Facebook's appeal could expand into more colleges and perhaps eventually into the general population.

Silicon Valley, California

Silicon Valley had an almost irresistible lure. As Mark told a reporter after he settled in California, "Palo Alto was kind of like this mythical place where all the techs used to come from. So I was like, I want to check that out."

However, Mark also wanted to move there for more practical reasons. He knew he would need help to make Facebook as exciting to the general population as it had been to college students, and a programming colleague named Andrew McCollum had a summer internship with Electronic Arts, a large interactive electronics company that created such popular video games as Madden NFL games, Sims, and Crysis. Mark hoped to enlist Andrew's help.

Andrew had been working on creating a software program with Mark at the time of the launch of Facebook. The program, which they called Wirehog, would allow friends to share content, similar to the legendary music-sharing site Napster. In addition to music, however, Wirehog would also allow the sharing of videos and other digital files. Now Mark also wanted it to connect to Facebook. That way a user's Facebook "friends" would be able to share content, which he thought would attract more users.

Electronic Arts was located in Redwood City, about a twenty-minute drive from Palo Alto. This would make it easy for Mark and Andrew to collaborate. After searching on another popular Web site, Craigslist.com, Mark found a small house to sublet for the summer: 819 La Jennifer Way was a four bedroom, three full bath ranch-style house. It also had a pool.

Mark knew he needed more help than Andrew to get Wirehog up and running. He convinced his friend Dustin to come out to California. He also hired two interns, Harvard freshmen Erik Schultink and Stephen Dawson-Haggerty, to work on more coding for Facebook, which would have to be much more robust if it was going to handle the amount of traffic he envisioned. Former roommate Chris Hughes was headed to

France to take part in a summer program, but promised to join the others as soon as he was finished. Eduardo, still very focused on trying to acquire revenue for the fledging company, opted not to go to Palo Alto, but to instead head to New York in order to better attract advertisers while he worked days at an investment firm.

In what looked like an Ivy League-type dorm transported from the East Coast, the house on La Jennifer Way became Facebook's first home. Computers, hard drives, cables, and other equipment covered what had been the dining room table. Mixed in among the working machinery were stray cups, soda cans, food wrappers, and various other trash. The place looked like an undergraduate men's dorm or fraternity house. However, there was serious work going on. They wrote code until late at night and would then sleep until late morning. Mark often walked around the house in pajama-type pants and one of his vast array of t-shirts.

Despite his very casual attire, it was clear that Mark was in charge and that Facebook was his baby. At the bottom of every Facebook page there was a tagline that read: "A Mark Zuckerberg production." On the Web site's "About" page, Mark was listed as "Founder, Master and Commander, Enemy of the State."

When they were all working, an almost creepy quiet descended upon the house that usually lasted for hours. When he wasn't writing code or thinking about how to do something through programming, Mark liked to watch movies. His tastes ran from larger-than-life films such as *Gladiator*, to the buddy/romantic comedy *The Wedding Crashers*. Mark had his fencing foils too and

Russel Crowe in *Gladiator*

often horsed around, thrusting them at the others like a swashbuckling Zorro. Eventually the other housemates banned Mark from carrying on his swordplay inside.

Nerds or not, Mark, Dustin, and the others were college guys who liked to have fun when they needed a break from programming. One afternoon Andrew got the idea of connecting a zip-line from the chimney of the house to a telephone pole across the yard. The zip-line hung directly over the pool, enabling whoever was riding down the cable to release over the water and make a huge splash. With Stanford University just a mile up the road from the house, parties were easy to pull together. A quick note posted on Facebook, which was available now at Stanford, was all that was needed. The parties were mostly the typical beer and alcohol fests. The guys played drinking games, including beer pong, and grilled hot dogs and steaks by the pool.

Although he liked to have an occasional good time, Mark was very antidrug and made it clear to his guests he didn't want to catch anyone smoking marijuana or using other drugs. This dictate got to be a bit more problematic for Mark after he invited Napster entrepreneur Sean Parker to move into the house on La Jennifer Way.

Mark had met Sean in New York City the previous spring. The evening dinner had been set up by Eduardo after he'd received an e-mail from Sean suggesting they meet to discuss the business side of Facebook. Mark, Priscilla, Eduardo, and his girlfriend met Sean in a restaurant in the city's chic Tribeca neighborhood. Sean dazzled Mark with his stories about raising large amounts of money for business ventures in California. In reality, Sean was not the wealthy, hip guy he projected himself to be. Napster, an online free music-sharing site, ran into copyright infringement legal troubles

Sean Parker

and was shut down in 2001. Sean co-founded another Internet company he named Plaxo, which he touted as "Your Address Book for Life." Raising capital for the business was easy, but Sean's slack work ethic and partying lifestyle left investors feeling uncomfortable. Eventually he was forced out of Plaxo by Sequoia Capital and Ram Shriram, a Google founding investor.

Mark and Sean had not seen each other until they bumped into each other one afternoon in Palo Alto. Mark was walking back from the grocery store. Sean was low on funds and had moved out of his apartment, which turned out to be only a block away from the Facebook headquarters. Mark invited Sean to come with him back to the house. At the end of the evening, which had been filled with tales of how Sean had been cheated by the Plaxo investors, Mark asked Sean to move in.

Mark was impressed with Sean's business sense and intellect and thought he might learn a lot from him. After all, at nineteen Sean had been a leader on the development of Napster; and by twenty had founded his own company. Mark knew writing code. He knew programming. He didn't think he had the business savvy that Sean had.

On some levels it was great to have Sean around. He was quickly addressing the legalities involved in formally transforming Facebook into a viable company.

Mark in 2009

He became the "face" of Facebook to potential investors. Also he was twenty-one, which meant he could legally purchase the beer and alcohol for the house parties. He also had a flashy BMW 5-series car which the others got to drive in exchange for a place to stay. By the end of the summer, Mark was referring to Sean as the company president. If Sean could focus on the business end of the company, Mark could spend his energies elsewhere. Since Eduardo was in New York seeking out what amounted to small advertising dollars, Mark was happy to have Sean looking for the large dollar infusion the company would need to keep Facebook alive.

For Mark, the main focus was how well Facebook functioned. Though content was important, speed of the delivery of each new page was crucial to keeping existing users and attracting new users. Continuing to upgrade existing equipment and buying new components was costing more than they had planned. Mark had already put in $20,000 of his own money since arriving in Palo Alto, and he was beginning to feel that Eduardo was not working hard enough to find investors. They clashed, and at one point Eduardo froze the checking account. Eduardo also fumed at Sean's involvement.

While Eduardo and Mark clashed, Sean was busy with a lawyer completely restructuring the company. Eventually Mark informed Eduardo through court filings that he was no longer an employee, citing as reasons his refusal to move to California and not producing the work he agreed to do. Eduardo's share in the company would also be reduced as new employees and investors came aboard.

Under the new incorporated company, Mark received 51 percent ownership, Eduardo got roughly 34 percent, and Dustin would receive almost 7 percent. New company president Sean Parker was given a 6.5 percent share. To keep Facebook going, Mark was still spending a lot of his own money, including $28,000 to buy twenty-five new servers. By the end of the summer, Facebook was reaching the 200,000-user milestone, and Mark and Dustin decided that they would not return to Harvard for the fall semester of their junior year.

The company was growing, but not everything was smooth sailing in California or back in Massachusetts. Owners of 819 La Jennifer Way returned to find their home a mess. Furniture had been damaged and the chimney needed repairs from the installment of the zip-line. More critically, on September 2, 2004, Divya.

Mark smiles in front of the blue Facebook logo at his office in Palo Alto, California, in 2007. He made Facebook's logo blue because he is red-green color-blind, which means he can see the color blue clearest.

Narendra, Cameron Winklevoss, and Tyler Winklevoss filed papers in United States District Court for the District of Massachusetts. They were suing Mark Zuckerberg for theft of their idea and his subsequent deception about their project, HarvardConnection (ConnectU).

Another problem was that money was running out. Facebook needed to acquire more capital to keep going. However, Mark was unyielding about maintaining complete control over Facebook's future. How to keep things going without compromising his control was becoming a real concern. The running and operation of Facebook was getting complicated, and it seemed there were more problems surfacing by the day.

Randi Zuckerberg

Soon after Mark made Facebook the primary focus of his young career, his sister Randi joined the staff as the director of marketing. She and Mark were close growing up, and she often had indulged and participated in Mark's practical jokes and grandiose projects. Randi was the first in the family to go to Harvard University; Mark entered his freshman year as Randi was finishing up her undergraduate degree in psychology. Randi is also a spokesperson for Facebook, and she has led "Facebook's U.S. election and international politics strategy, in addition to managing media partnerships with companies such as ABC News and CNN."

Randi Zuckerberg speaks during a social networking session at the opening day of the World Economic Forum in Davos, Switzerland, in January 2010.

CHAPTER
SIX

The World's Biggest Social Network

Despite the need for a nearly constant infusion of money to keep Facebook up and running, Mark was firm about not selling it to outside interests. The cable music giant MTV considered offering $75 million to buy the company. Microsoft let it be known they were interested as well. Mark turned them down. In an interview with *Fortune* magazine, he said, "I'm in this to build something cool, not to get bought."

Terry Semel, former chief executive officer of Yahoo!, offered $1 billion to buy Facebook. Mark rejected the offer. Said Semel, "I'd never met anyone—forget his age, twenty-two then or twenty-six now—I'd never met anyone who would walk away from a billion dollars. But he said, 'It's not about the price. This is my baby, and I want to keep running it, I want to keep growing it.' I couldn't believe it."

Terry Semel in 2005

Facebook was growing rapidly. By December 2004, it had almost 1 million daily users. In mid-2005 a new feature had been added to the Facebook page. The wall enabled users to post messages for their friends.

Because they had trashed the rented house at 819 La Jennifer Way, Facebook had to find another headquarters. This time they moved the operation into a brand new home in Los Altos Hills. A few miles south of Palo Alto, the house's yard backed up to Interstate 280. Whatever noise the boys would make when they had a party couldn't be heard over the traffic, which was a good thing.

The house was trashed in no time. They had little concern about hygiene. Unwashed dishes piled up in the kitchen sink, and the trash was rarely put out for pick-up. Where the equipment resided was no better. Wires were strung in a maze, and laptops and papers were tossed everywhere. The messiness, or lack of furniture, didn't interfere with the work they did building the world's largest social networking site.

Sean Parker finally found a big investor. Peter Thiel was the founder of PayPal, an e-commerce business that allows payments to be made through the Internet. He agreed to loan the company $500,000 and further agreed that if Facebook reached 1.5 million users before December 31, 2004, the loan would convert to an investment, giving Thiel a 10.2 percent share in the company. This would mean the money would not have to be paid back.

By November 2004 Facebook had registered its millionth user. It was costing about $50,000 a month to cover the operating costs, and Mark figured they would need about $100,000 to buy more servers. He agreed to sell 15 percent of the company to the venture capital firm Accel for a $12.7 million investment. Despite the need to sell interest in the company to raise money, Mark still held onto control by maintaining two seats on the Facebook board while Sean, Peter, and Jim Breyer, from Accel, each had one.

With money worries behind him for a while, Mark, Dustin, Sean, and Yale graduate Matt Cohler focused on growing Facebook. In February 2005 they moved the company again, this time to a small space above a Chinese restaurant. At that time their chief Internet competitor was MySpace. Mark was determined to overtake MySpace's lead in number of users. To attain his goal Mark opened up Facebook registration to high school students in September 2005 and to the international school community in October. In a continuing effort to improve the features of the Facebook site, in November the Web site introduced an application that enabled users to upload photos.

Facebook began to operate more like a structured company. They hired engineers and more programmers and defined roles and responsibilities. Netscape Communications co-founder Marc Andreesen, who has

cc - Eirik Solheim - www.eirikso.com

Sean Parker, left, and Matt Cohler in 2008

become a legend in Silicon Valley by creating the first popular web browser, became a regular visitor and later a close adviser to Mark. Robin Reed, a well-regarded employee recruiter agreed to work with Mark to find a vice president of engineering. Kevin Efrusy, the man who had landed the Accel deal, was also a frequent face around the office.

When Mark finally agreed to permit advertising to be sold on Facebook, Tricia Black from the advertising firm Y2M set up a fully functional advertising department. She hired Kevin Colleran as Facebook's new ad salesman.

The first major advertiser was Party Poker, a British online gaming company. Party Poker paid a three hundred dollar flat fee for each new Facebook subscriber who joined the gaming site and deposited at least fifty dollars into their gambling account. Before online gambling was banned in the United States in September of 2006, Party Poker brought in about $60,000 a month to Facebook. The most lucrative advertiser in 2005 was Apple Computer. It was one of Facebook's "sponsored groups," "which let companies buy a link from the Facebook sign-in landing page to a sponsored 'group page' that contains ad copy and a message board." Apple was paying one dollar per month per member, so revenues increased as the group grew.

Perhaps the only bad news of the year for Facebook centered around Sean Parker. Still living life in the fast lane, he was arrested, and later released, for suspicion of possession of cocaine during a party at his rented house in North Carolina. Mark was not as concerned as others at Facebook about the arrest. However, some of the investors feared the news could tarnish the image of the company. Board member and Accel representative

Jim Breyer was adamant that Sean had to go. After a few days of discussion between Mark, Sean, and company legal counsel Steve Venuto, Parker resigned as president. He assigned his seat on the board to Mark, ensuring that his friend would never have his control of the company compromised. Although Sean was out as a company director, Mark continued to consult with him.

By the fall of 2005 Facebook was being accessed by about 85 percent of college students in the United States. By the end of the year Facebook reached a milestone that had once been considered unattainable—5.5 million registered users. Throughout 2006, the Facebook site continued to see additions and modifications, including a mobile feature that allowed users to receive full messages, pokes, wall-posts, and friend requests wherever they were. In September, Mark agreed to open Facebook membership to anyone over the age of thirteen with a valid e-mail address.

One added feature caused a great deal of negative reactions. The company decided to add a news feed that would appear on each user's home page. The news feed put each users information, such as profile changes, upcoming events, and the birthdays of their friends, on their homepage. Many Facebook users were initially unhappy with the addition of the news feed because

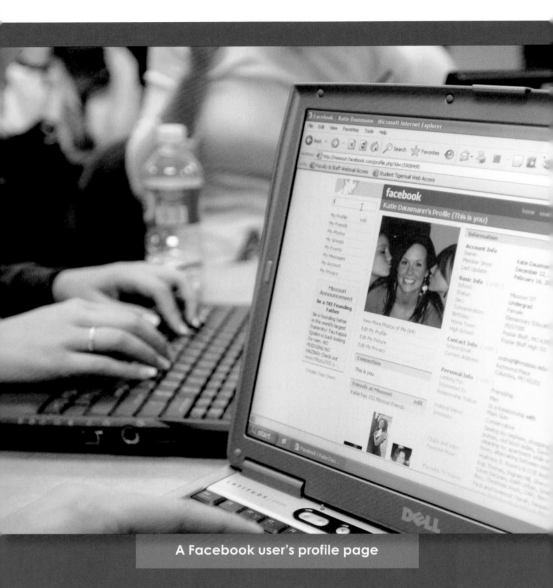

A Facebook user's profile page

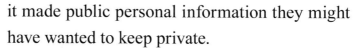

it made public personal information they might have wanted to keep private.

Negative reactions to the news feed poured in. Only one out of a hundred of the messages were positive. The staff had not been prepared for such a reaction. Mark, the biggest proponent of global openness, was the first to see the irony of the outrage. For him, it demonstrated that news feed was working. Protest groups formed on the site. Ben Parr, a junior at Northwestern University, created the anti-news feed group "Students Against Facebook news feed." He wrote: "You went a bit too far this time, Facebook. Very few of us want everyone automatically knowing what we update . . . news feed is just too creepy, too stalker-esque, and a feature that has to go."

As he absorbed the angry reactions, Mark began to realize that they had failed to communicate to users why the company thought the news feed was a positive addition to Facebook. He issued an apology on the Facebook Blog: "We really messed this one up. When we launched News Feed and Mini-Feed we were trying to provide you with a stream of information about your social world. Instead, we did a bad job of explaining what the new features were and an even worse job of giving you control of them." A set of privacy features were added to the site so users could set the controls to suit their comfort zone. The outrage died down. Facebook had survived its first major user crisis.

At the end of 2006 Facebook was being accessed by more than 12 million users across the country. The company employed 130 people. Yahoo! returned with its $1 billion offer. This time Mark agonized over his decision. It was a lot of money for him as well as for some of the people who worked for him who owned stock. They would become instant millionaires. Ultimately, he turned down the offer because he believed the company had the opportunity to change millions of lives. The continual rise in registration indicated to him that Facebook was doing something important that affected the lives of millions of people, and he wanted to continue to be a part of it.

By the fall of 2007, almost half of the users on Facebook were outside the United States and the number of total users topped 50 million worldwide. To accommodate their international "friends," Facebook launched its sites in Spanish, French, and German.

A screen shot of Facebook's privacy policy section

On October 24, 2007, an announcement was released from the corporate offices of Microsoft. It had just completed the purchase of a 1.6 percent share of Facebook for $240 million. In 2008, Facebook announced the opening of its international offices in Dublin, Ireland. The 100-million user mark was reached in August of the same year. 2008 is also the year Mark finally settled the lawsuit filed by Divya Narendra and twin brothers

Cameron and Tyler Winklevoss. Sixty-five million in a combination of stock and cash was awarded to the three after the court ruled in their favor.

In July 2009 a book written by author Ben Mezrich was published about Mark Zuckerberg and the founding of Facebook. The book was titled *The Accidental Billionaires: The Founding of Facebook, A Tale of Sex, Money, Genius, and Betrayal.* A motion picture adaptation of the book, *The Social Network,* was released in theaters on October 1, 2010. The book was a success and the film received critical acclaim, earning eight Academy Award nominations and taking home three, including one for best adapted screenplay. At the sixty-eighth Golden Globe Awards on January 16, 2011, the film won the Best Motion Picture Drama, as well as awards for Best Director, Best Screenplay, and Best Original Film Score.

Whether the film was factually accurate has been the subject of debate among those who knew Mark, the Winklevoss brothers, and Divya Narendra. Mark's contention is that it isn't an accurate portrayal of the founding of Facebook.

Although there had been a settlement, the Winklevoss brothers filed a new suit requesting that the monetary payout they received be reviewed. They believed the value of the stock they had received was undervalued, which lowered their settlement. Now they wanted it reviewed in hopes it would be increased. On April 11, 2011, Ninth U.S. Circuit Court of Appeals Chief Judge Alex Kozinski rejected the suit, citing the need for all litigations to come to an end at some point.

Mark's legal troubles did not end with the rejection of the Winklevoss's lawsuit. Two other former Harvard students filed suits claiming they own the rights to the Internet giant. The publicity from the book, movie, and lawsuits have not negatively impacted the popularity of the Web site. As of February 2011, Facebook exceeded 650 million users.

A scene from *The Social Network*

CHAPTER SEVEN

Facebook's Global Influence

Mark Zuckerberg was named *Time* magazine's 2010 Person of the Year. According to managing editor Richard Stengel, the selection of Person of the Year has never been an endorsement of the person chosen. Writes Stengel:

> It is a recognition of the power of individuals to shape our world. For connecting more than half a billion people and mapping the social relations among them (something that has never been done before); for creating a new system of exchanging

Person *of the* Year

TIME

**Facebook's
Mark
Zuckerberg**

THE CONNECTOR

www.time.com

Time magazine's cover
featuring Mark as Person of the Year

information that has become both indispensable and sometimes a little scary; and finally, for changing how we all live our lives in ways that are innovative and even optimistic, Mark Elliot Zuckerberg is *TIME*'s 2010 Person of the Year.

Stengel and the editors at *Time* could not have known how accurately they had described Facebook's potential.

On Tuesday, January 25, 2011, thousands of Egyptians flooded the streets in the capital city of Cairo to protest the continued poverty, extensive unemployment, and government oppression that had existed for more than thirty years under the country's president, Hosni Mubarek. The unrest and oftentimes violent protests went on for eighteen days. On February 11, Mubarek finally resigned and left Cairo. What was different about this revolt than ones that had happened previously in other countries was the role Facebook played in helping the protestors.

Not long after Mubarek's resignation, Egyptian activist Wael Ghonim told CNN reporter Wolf Blitzer that Facebook was the reason the uprising had been so successful. "Earlier this year, Ghonim—anonymously—launched a Facebook page commemorating

Khaled Said, a 28-year-old businessman in Alexandria who was beaten to death by two policemen in June. The page became a rallying point for a campaign against police brutality, with hundreds of thousands joining. For many Egyptians, it was the first time to learn details of the extent of widespread torture in their own country."

Ghomin's page was the "information channel" for getting plans for protests out to the thousands who participated. Two days after the unrest began, Ghonim was arrested and thrown into jail. However, the other protest organizers used Ghomin's page to continue to share strategies and ideas. "When we say let's organize a protest, let's think, five people sit together and plan. Imagine now 50,000 heads are put together through the Internet. Lots of creativity and greatness," said another leader of the protests 'Ghomin has been called a hero, but he says the people who flooded the streets in protest are the real heroes. He merely sat at a keyboard out of harms' way while others put their lives in jeopardy by taking to the streets.

After the revolt was successful in toppling the Egyptian government, Ghomin said he had a wish. "I want to meet Mark Zuckerberg one day and thank him. . . . I'm talking on behalf of Egypt. This revolution started online. This revolution started on Facebook.

This revolution started in June 2010 when hundreds of thousands of Egyptians started collaborating content. We would post a video on Facebook that would be shared by 60,000 people on their walls within a few hours. I've always said that if you want to liberate a society just give them the Internet."

Though Facebook representatives downplayed the social network's role in the successful uprising, its use was a prime example of what Mark Zuckerberg espouses:

> The thing I really care about is making the world more open and connected. What that stands for is something that I have believed in for a really long time. . . . Open means having access to more information, right? More transparency, being able to share things and have a voice in the world. And connected is helping people stay in touch and maintain empathy for each other.

In his article about the uprising, "Egypt, the Age of Disruption and the 'Me' in Media," Jose Antonio Vargas of the *New Yorker* wrote:

An anti-Mubarak protester holds a sign praising Facebook for helping to organize the protest in Tahrir Square in Cairo, Egypt.

But what's proving more consequential than access to information is our growing access to one another, human-to-human, enabled by the Internet and mobile tools. As the author Clay Shirky has consistently and presciently said: 'We have historically overestimated the value of access to information and underestimated the value of access to one another.' Enter Facebook. As the unprecedented directory of the world's people, it's the social-networking site most explicitly tied to our individual and collective identities—a site where every private citizen has a public identity.

Facebook is quickly expanding beyond what was considered to be the role of a social media site. According to Facebook's own statistics, their users spend more than 700 billion minutes per month on Facebook; there are more than 200 million active users currently accessing Facebook through their mobile devices.

In statistics released in the spring of 2011, an astonishing 1,789,736 actions were performed on Facebook every 60 seconds. 510,404 comments were posted,

231,605 messages sent, 135,849 photos added, and 79,364 wall posts written.

Well before he reached the age of thirty, Mark Zuckerberg had made a global impact few rarely achieve. Facebook employs more than 2,000 people and has offices in fifteen countries. Mark, despite being a multibillionaire, does not live a lavish life. He drives a modest car and in May 2011 bought his first house, after renting for years. He is still in a relationship with Priscilla Chan.

Mark apparently has no plans to resign from Facebook. He has always contended that he will stay with the company he founded as long as it is changing people's lives. If that is true, he will probably continue to lead the company he founded for a long time.

Mark Zuckerberg in 2008

1984   Born May 14 in White Plains, New York.

1995   Begins taking computer tutoring lessons from software developer David Newman; takes a graduate computer course weekly at Mercy College.

1996   Creates ZuckNet for his father's dental office.

1997   Celebrates his thirteenth birthday in the Jewish tradition by having his Bar Mitzvah.

1998   Attends Ardsley High school for his freshman and sophomore years.

2000   Transfers to Phillips Exeter Academy, in Exeter, New Hampshire.

2002   For senior school project, writes the software to a program he calls Synapse Media Player to learn users musical listening habits; enters the freshmen class at Harvard University, in Cambridge, Massachusetts.

2003   Creates CourseMatch, a software program that compared similar courses at Harvard.

2004   Writes the code for Thefacebook.com, an earlier name for the now famous Facebook; co-founds Facebook with roommates Dustin Moskovitz, Chris Hughes, and Eduardo Saverin.

2007   Announces the creation of Facebook Platform, "a standards-based Web service with methods for accessing and contributing Facebook data."

2009   Attends the World Economic Forum in Davos, Switzerland.

2010   Facebook hits the 500 million-user mark; donates $100 million to improve public schools in Newark, New Jersey, *The Social Network*, released; named *Time*'s 2010 Person of the Year.

2011   Becomes first-time homeowner with the purchase of a $7 million house in Palo Alto; house is a ten-minute drive from Facebook's soon-to-be new corporate campus in Menlo Park.

Chapter One: **Techno Kid**

pp. 11-12, "strong willed and relentless . . ." Lev Grossman, "2010 Person of the Year," *Time*, December 15, 2010.

p. 14, "I've always been technologically oriented . . . " Edward Zuckerberg, interview by Paul Feiner (Greenburgh Town Supervisor, Greenburg, New York), February 18, 2011, "Interview with Facebook Founder Mark Zuckerberg's Dad," Student News Network, http://www.snnews.org/wp-content/uploads/2011/02/Zuckerberg1S.mp3.

Chapter Two: **More than Just a Geek**

p.22, "I had a bunch of friends . . ." Jose Antonio Vargas, "The Face of Facebook," *New Yorker*, September 20, 2010.

p. 23, "Probably the best . . ." Edward Zuckerberg, interview by Paul Feiner.

p. 28, "software for an MP3 . . ." Claire Hoffman, "The Battle for Facebook," *Rolling Stone*, September 15, 2010.

p. 28, "The playlist ran out . . ." Michael Grynbaum, "Mark E. Zuckerberg '06: The Whiz Behind Thefacebook.com," *Harvard Crimson*, June 10, 2004.

p. 29, "I don't really like . . ." Ibid.

pp. 29-30, "proven to be the perfect . . ." Hoffman, "The Battle for Facebook."

Chapter Three: **Hacking Harvard**

p. 34, "I'm just like a little kid . . ." Grynbaum, "Mark E. Zuckerberg '06: The Whiz Behind Thefacebook.com."

p. 38, "Half the things I do . . ." Ibid.

pp. 38-39, "is to provide every Jewish . . ." Official Web site of Harvard Hillel, http://hillel.harvard.edu/about-us/harvard-hillels-mission.

p. 39, "their friends and compared..." David Kirkpatrick, "The Social Network: A Misleading View of Facebook's Birth," *Telegraph* (UK), October 14, 2010, http://www.telegraph.co.uk/technology/facebook/8063401/The-Social-Network-a-misleading-view-of-Facebooks-birth.html.

p. 40 "Jessica A— is a bitch . . ." Hoffman, "The Battle for Facebook."

p. 42,   "Zuckerberg hacked . . ." Ibid.

p. 43,   "People are more . . ." Ibid.

Chapter Four: **Whose Idea Was It?**

p. 45,   "He was this nerdy guy . . ." Jose Antonio Vargas, "The Face of Facebook," *New Yorker*, September 20, 2010.

p. 46,   "This isn't the kind . . . " Ellen McGirt, "Hacker. Dropout. CEO.," *Fast Company*, May 1, 2007, http://www.fastcompany.com/magazine/115/open_features-hacker-dropout-ceo_2.html.

p. 49,   "All three of us . . ." Luke O'Brien, "Poking Facebook," InformationLiberation, December 3, 2007, http://www.informationliberation.com/?id=24402.

p. 49,   "We're very deep into . . ." Ibid.

p. 50,   "I have most of . . . " Ibid.

p. 51,   "Thefacebook is an online . . ." David Kirkpatrick, *The Facebook Effect* (New York: Simon and Schuster, 2010), 30.

p. 52,   "Mark came to me on . . ." Guy Grimland, "Facebook Founder's Roommate Recounts Creation of Internet Giant," Haaretz.com, October 5, 2009, http://www.haaretz.com/news/facebook-founder-s-roommate-recounts-creation-of-internet-giant-1.275748.

p. 54,   "Originally, I was intrigued . . ." "Facebook accused of stealing idea," *Daily Free Press* (Boston University), September 9, 2004, http://dailyfreepress.com/2004/09/09/facebook-accused-of-stealing-idea-2/.

p. 54,   "Mark's 'work' on the site . . ." Ibid.

pp. 54-55, "expects that all students . . ." Ibid.

p. 56,   "claiming Zuckerberg stole . . ." Ibid.

Chapter Five: **Palo Alto: A "Mythical Place"**

p. 61,   "While facebook.com isn't . . ." Kirkpatrick, *The Facebook Effect*, 33.

p. 62,   "Palo Alto was kind . . ." Ibid., 44.

p. 64,   "A Mark Zuckerberg production," Ibid., 52

Chapter Six: **The World's Biggest Social Network**

p. 77,   "I'm in this to build . . ." Hoffman, "The Battle for Facebook."

p. 78,   "I'd never met anyone . . ." Vargas, "The Face of Facebook."

p. 82,   "which let companies buy . . ." Justin Smith, "Brand advertising programs at Facebook and Myspace Working," Inside Facebook. com, http://www.insidefacebook.com/2006/05/22/brand-adver- tising-is-the-crux-of-the-social-networking-business/.

p. 85,   "You went a bit too . . ." Kirkpatrick, *The Facebook Effect*, 190.

pp. 85-86,   "We really messed this . . ." Mark Zuckerberg, "An Open Letter from Mark Zuckerberg," September 8, 2006, http://blog.face- book.com/blog.php?post=2208562130.

Chapter Seven: **Facebook's Global Influence**

pp. 93-95,   "It is a recognition . . . " Richard Stengel, "Only Connect," *Time*, December 27, 2010-January 3, 2011.

pp. 95-96,   "Earlier this year . . ." Sarah El Deeb and Maggie Michael, "Wael Ghonim, Freed Activist, Energizes Egyptian Protests," Associated Press, Huffpost World, February 8, 2011, http:// www.huffingtonpost.com/2011/02/08/wael-ghonim-freed- activis_n_820290.html.

p. 96,   "When we say let's . . ." Ibid.

pp. 96-97,   "I want to meet Mark . . ." Catherine Smith, "Egypt's Facebook Revolution: Wael Ghonim Thanks The Social Network," Huff Post Technology, http://www.huffingtonpost.com/2011/02/11/ egypt-facebook-revolution-wael-ghonim_n_822078.html.

p. 97,   "The thing I really care . . ." Grossman, "2010 Person of the Year."

p. 100,   "But what's proving more . . ." Jose Antonio Vargas, "Egypt, the Age of Disruption and the 'Me' in Media," Huffington Post, February 7, 2011, http://joseantoniovargas.com/2011/02/07/ egypt-the-age-of-disruption-and-the-me-in-media/.

Kirkpatrick, David. *The Facebook Effect*. New York: Simon and Schuster, 2010.

———. "The Social Network: A Misleading View of Facebook's Birth." *Telegraph* (UK), October 14, 2010. http://www.telegraph.co.uk/technology/facebook/8063401/ The-Social-Network-a-misleading-view-of-Facebooks-birth.html.

Garfield, Simon. "So How Many Friends Do You Have, Mark?" *Observer* (UK), November 16, 2008. http://www.guardian.co.uk/media/2008/nov/16/mark-zuckerberg-facebook-social-networking.

Grossman, Lev. "2010 Person of the Year." *Time*, December 15, 2010.

Grynbaum, Michael. "Mark E. Zuckerberg '06: The Whiz Behind Thefacebook.com." *Harvard Crimson*, June 10, 2004.

Hoffman, Claire. "The Battle for Facebook." *Rolling Stone*, September 15, 2010.

McGirt, Ellen. "Hacker. Dropout. CEO." *Fast Company*, May 1, 2007. http://www.fastcompany.com/magazine/115/open_features-hacker-dropout-ceo_2.html.

Vargas, Jose Antonio. "The Face of Facebook." *New Yorker*, September 20, 2010.

———. "Egypt, the Age of Disruption and the 'Me' in Media." Huffington Post, February 7, 2011. http://joseantoniovargas.com/2011/02/07/egypt-the-age-of-disruption-and-the-me-in-media/.

———. "Mark Zuckerberg-Our First Millennial CEO." Huffington Post, December 9, 2010.

Woog, Adam. *Mark Zuckerberg: Facebook Creator*. Farmington Hills, MI: Kidhaven Press, 2009.

Harvard Crimson: "Facebooks Duel Over Tangled Web."
http://www.thecrimson.
comarticle/2004/5/28online-facebooks-duel-over-tangled-web/

Mark Zuckerberg's Official Facebook page
http://www.facebook.com/home.php#!/markzuckerberg

Mark Zuckerberg's Personal Facebook Page
http://www.facebook.com/search.php?q=Priscilla%20Chan%20medical%20stude
nt&init=quick&tas=0.5408993485516753&search_first_focus=1302398059523#!/
zuck

Facebook History
http://ifacebook.org/facebook.html

Accel, 80-82
Alpha Epsilon Pi, 35-36, 38, *38*
Andreesen, Marc, 80-81
AOL, 28-29
Apple Computer, 57, 82

BASIC (computer program), 14-15
Black, Tricia, 81-82
Breyer, Jim, 80, 82-83
Buddy Zoo, 39

Chan, Priscilla, 45, 67, 101
Classmates.com, 58
Cohler, Matt, 80, *81*
Colleran, Kevin, 82
ConnectU, 55, 74
Conrads, Randy, 58
CourseMatch, 39-40

D'Angelo, Adam, 28-29, 39
Dawson-Haggerty, Stephen, 63

Efrusy, Kevin, 81
Egypt, 95-97, *98-99,* 100
Electronic Arts, 62-63

Facebook, *72-73, 84-85, 87*
    advertisements, 70-71, 81-82
    beginnings, 12, 40-43, 47-52
    development and growth, 63-65, 78, 80
    expansion needs, 53-54, 70-71, 78
    features, 63, 70, 78, 80, 82-83, 85-86
    financial issues, 53-54, 64, 70-71, 74, 77-80, 82, 86
    impact of, 95-97, 100
    incorporation, 71
    international business, 80, 86-87
    investors, 70-71, 79-80
    legal issues, 53-57, 74, 82-83, 87-89
    management of, 64, 70-71, 74, 80, 83, 101
    marketing, 75, 81-82
    media recognition, 88
    popularity, 61, 71, 78-79, 83, 86, 100-101
    privacy issues, 83, 85-86
    social atmosphere, 64, 66, 78-79
    technical aspects, 70-71, 79-80
    users, 51-53, 61-62, 66, 78-80, 83, 86-87, 89, 100-101
    website launched, 50-52

Facemash.com, 41-42, 47
Friendster, 58-59

Gao, Victor, 49-50, 54
Gates, Bill, 18, 57
Ghomin, Wael, 95-97, 100

Harvard Connection, 49-50, 53-55, 74
Harvard Honor Code, 54-55
Hasit, Arie, 38, 51-52
Hughes, Chris, 36, 51, 53, 63

LinkedIn, 58-59

McCollum, Andrew, 62-63, 66
Memory Lane, 58
Mezrich, Ben, 88
Microsoft, 29, 57, 77, 87
Moscovitz, Dustin, 36, 51, 53, 63, 71, 80
MTV, 77
Mubarek, Hosni, 95-97, 100
MySpace, 80

Napster, 63, 66-68
Narendra, Divya, 47-50, *47,* 53-57, 74, 87-88
Netscape Communications, 80
Newman, David, 23
Nintendo, 21, *22*

Olsen, Billy, 41

Pandora, 28
Parker, Sean, 66-68, *67,* 70, 71, 79-80, *81,* 82-83
Parr, Ben, 85
Party Poker, 82
PayPal, 79
Phillips Exeter Academy, 24-26, 29-30
Plaxo, 67-68

Quantex 486DX computer, 15

Said, Khaled, 96
Saverin, Eduardo, 36, 51, 53, 64, 67, 70-71
Schultink, Erik, 63
Sega, 21
Semel, Terry, 78, *78*
Sequoia Capital, 68

Shriram, Ram, 68
social networking, 39-40, 46, 48-52, 58-59, 95-97, 100
Summers, Lawrence, 55, *55*
Synapse, 28-29, 31

The Accidental Billionaires, 88
TheFacebook.com, 50-51, 55
The Social Network, 88, *90-91*
Thiel, Peter, 79-80
Tillery, Kristopher, 28
Time Magazine, 93, 95

Venuto, Steve, 83

Wii, 21
Winklevoss, Cameron, 47-50, *47,* 53-57, *56,* 74, 87-89
Winklevoss, Tyler, 47-50, *47,* 53-57, *56,* 74, 87-89
Wirehog, 63

Yahoo!, 78, 86
Y2K bug, 16-18
Y2M, 82

Zuckerberg, Arielle (sister), 12, 24
Zuckerberg, Donna (sister), 12, 16, 24
Zuckerberg, Edward (father), 11-16, 18-19, 23
Zuckerberg, Karen (mother), 11-13, 16, 18-19, 23
Zuckerberg, Mark, *6-7, 53, 69, 72-73, 94, 102*
    character, 11, 16-19, 22, 35, 45
    childhood and youth, 12-16, 21-24
    and computer programming, 15-16, 24, 28-29, 31, 35, 38-39, 41-42,
        46, 63
    education, 22, 24-26, 28-30, 71
    and fencing, 26, 29-30, 65-66
    Harvard years, 29-31, 33-36, 38-40, 45-46
    honors and awards, 16, 93, 95
    influences, 22, 24
    as a Jew, 24, 35-36, 38-39
    lawsuit, 54-57, 87-89
    media recognition, 88, 93, 95
    philosophies, 12, 97
    and technology, 14-16, 21-22, 24, 31, 34
Zuckerberg, Randi (sister), 12, 18, 21, 24, 75, *75*
Zucknet, 16, 28, 31

All images used in this book not in the public domain are credited in the listing that follows: